RECONCILING THROUGH LOVE

LEARN | CONNECT | LOVE   RealLifeRelationships.org

Illustrations hand drawn by Beth Rampelberg

ISBN 978-1-7331443-3-9

Life is a journey we are all on together. We don't always get to choose what happens along life's journey. Life, in itself, is a series of events. Those events can be good or not so good, some could even be seen as great and others as traumatic. We do have choices about how we respond to what has happened throughout life. Everyone at some point reconciles certain events in life. Life is not perfect since it involves people who are not perfect and an imperfect world.

Reconciling Through Love is a self-guided course intended to help individuals work toward reconciling life to a "right place". What that "right place" is, and what the rest of an individual's life looks like, is still being determined.

Reconciling Through

Looking at past negative life events, while

Opening your heart, mind and soul to healing in the present.

Valuing yourself, and the parts of your life still yet to be lived,

Enough to find FAITH, HOPE and LOVE again in the future.

When "life" happens, three things remain regardless of current circumstances; faith, hope and love with the greatest of these being love.

Relationship Education is not therapy, it is an educational process. PREP Inc. has 35 plus years of research, data and work related to the field of Relationship Education. Their research and work has helped thousands of individuals and couples worldwide learn how to better preserve and protect relationships in areas of communication, problem discussion, resolution, and commitment. Visit their website at PREPINC.com to learn more.

Real Life Relationships self-guided course books are not a substitute for therapy. Real Life Relationships educational course books are written and created to allow individuals and couples to self-evaluate life and relationships. Visit our website at RealLifeRelationships.org to learn more about all of our relationship education self-guided course books and the book *Love Forever*.

The concepts and exercises in this self-guided course have been written and created in the same format used in Relationship Education. We personally connect in life through events and relationships. We keep connecting in life, as we reconcile relationships and life events, throughout our lifetime.

FINDING FAITH, HOPE, AND LOVE AGAIN

One way we reconcile life is by letting go of the pain that has been caused from experiencing something negative in life. One term used to describe the process of letting go and moving forward after a negative life event is called **Post Traumatic Growth.** This concept refers to the process of moving toward reconciliation after experiencing something we can't forget or change. Life can be difficult. Persevering during the trials of life is not necessarily something we like, but it is something we need to do at different times in life. The endurance we gain, the resilience we have, and our ability to thrive afterwards allows us to see just how strong we really are.

As stated in the introduction, throughout life, regardless of circumstances, we can work toward having and experiencing three things: faith, hope and love. Sometimes if we can just catch a glimpse of what the future could look like, others can begin to help us work toward that new vision of life. That new vision may become clearer as we decide to work through negative life events.

Exercise One: In the following exercise, think about past or present events that have impacted your life. Complete the following statements by writing about any thoughts and/or decisions you are considering regarding those life events and your thoughts about the future.

In faith, I want to _____

_____

_____

Out of hope for the future, currently I can _____

_____

_____

Because of love for myself and those who love me, I will _____

_____

_____

REFLECTIONS OF LIFE

Each of our lives tell a different story, that story has many different chapters. Everyone faces, and will face, trials throughout life. Some trials are because of choices we make, others are because of someone else's choices, and even more are a result of unplanned events or unexpected disappointments that were not predictable. Everyone's trials are different, yet each one has an impact. How we view the trial, the length of the trial, the lasting impact of the trial, and even how we reconcile toward a new normal, is an individual journey. As we begin working toward a "right place" it is important to see what reflections (negative life events) from our past are still affecting us.

Exercise One: Write about any negative life events from your past which are still affecting your view of life today and your hope of a new tomorrow? Examples: painful memories, significant losses, personal regrets, abuse (physical, emotional, sexual), addictions, relationship failures, other negative life experiences.

_____

_____

_____

_____

_____

Sometimes the reflections of our life can be discouraging. At times we may be so discouraged that we can't even see a ray of light shining through the darkness of our present situation. The darkness is a negative reflection. Negative reflections can be distorted images or discouraging thoughts and feelings. These thoughts, images and feelings may be ideas and responses you currently have or perceive about yourself and your life.

Exercise Two: Circle any negative thoughts you have or perceive about yourself and your future because of past negative life experiences.

I have no hope   I cannot forgive myself   Nothing will ever change   I cannot truly love

I trust the wrong people   I cannot change   I will never be good enough   I cannot heal

My opinions do not matter   I cannot succeed   I am not safe   No one will ever love me

I cannot forgive other people   My life is broken beyond repair   I cannot trust anyone

I do not make good decisions   My past cannot be reconciled   I will never be whole again

Exercise Three: On the lines provided below, write any phrases you circled from the previous page. Next to each phrase, write about the negative life experience you associate with the negative thought you have about yourself and/or your life.

_____

_____

_____

_____

_____

_____

Hold on to hope, while letting go of hurt and a past you can't change.

It may sometimes appear to be easier to focus on what we have lost in the past rather than looking toward what could be in the future. Each day is a new day. The reflections we see regarding the past will continue to change.

LOVE OF SELF

Looking at past reflections of our life can sometimes help give us glimpses of how different our life is today. Recognizing problems that need to be solved, and identifying issues that need reconciliation is part of the process of moving toward a new normal after a negative life event. Anytime we attempt to resolve something we must define what specifically needs resolution. Understanding how life events have affected our thoughts and feelings helps us to better understand what we are reconciling. Looking for all possibilities of how to resolve or reconcile toward a new future may also help us to develop a plan that leads us toward a future "right place" we decide in the future.

Exercise One: Re-examine the statements you circled in the last exercise. On the lines provided, write positive statements that you hope could replace the negative thoughts you currently believe. The statements you write are new visions you have for yourself and your life in the future.

Below is an example of how to turn a negative statement into a hopeful thought for the future.

If you circled, *I have no hope,* you could work toward replacing that thought with...
Even though I currently do not feel hopeful, I can work toward seeing hope in small areas of my life as I continue to heal.

_____

_____

_____

_____

_____

_____

_____

Sometimes replacing negative thoughts with new thoughts can help us envision a future we can work toward. Reconciling past negative life events and trials in life is possible but the time and effort it takes to reconcile is different for everyone.

Love is patient, love yourself enough to be patient as you struggle to see and work toward an unknown future.

LETTING GO OF FAILURE

Each chapter of life will hopefully have some successes and most likely will also have some failures. Failure lasts for a period of time, it does not last a lifetime. Why? Because we can always start over. Failure is one of many types of trials we will face throughout life.

We all experience failure, sometimes because of our own actions, and other times as a consequence of someone else's. Sometimes failure is just a part of life. Failure is related to an event, it is not a person. Failure is a fact of life, not a way of life. After failure there is always a new starting point, it is sometimes referred to as a new beginning.

Exercise One: In this exercise you have an opportunity to view failure as a part of life and also envision how to have success in the future. First, list any significant failures from the past that have had an impact on your life. Next, list any success you are planning toward or any visions of success you view as being a possibility in the future. Use the notes section at the back of this course book if you need additional space.

Failures of the past	New Beginnings/Future Success

Success in the future can sometimes be influenced by our belief of self-worth. Recognizing self-worth allows an individual to see value of life and self. Self-value is partially rooted in someone's individual idea of what success is.

Success is not only measured by others, or only on a monetary scale. Success is also measured through the eyes of the one striving toward a certain idea of success.

Consider the following statement. ***Grace is available to all of us, it starts with forgiving a past we can't change and a choosing a future that is good.***

Exercise Two: Write a sentence regarding how you could apply this idea to your life, as you continue to look toward the future.

_____

_____

TRUTH ABOUT YOUR LIFE

Previous exercises pertained to negative reflections, thoughts and beliefs about self, and unexpected failures. Each of those exercises were designed to help link events in the past to thoughts and feelings in the present.

The past events written about in those exercises can affect how you think about life and your view of life in general. In this next exercise, you will be looking at how events and trials in life have shaped some of the beliefs you have about life in general today.

Exercise One: Based on the statements below what did you believe before negative life experiences and trials in life? Circle what you believed at one time.

Before a negative life experience, I believed:

I am safe	The world is good
I am "OK"	Life is positive
I can trust most people	I am loved

Exercise Two: Based on the statements below, what do you currently believe about yourself and your life? Circle what you believe now.

After a negative life experience or trial in life I now believe:

I am not safe	I am not loveable
The world is evil	Life is negative
I can't trust anyone	I am broken

Exercise Three: After looking at both lists and circling your answers what did you learn about your beliefs in the past versus your beliefs today? Write about anything that comes to mind regarding this exercise that you didn't realize before or are just beginning to process now. Use the following lead-in statement to help you start writing:

Since going through negative life experiences and trials of life I see life in general as...

_____

_____

_____

_____

_____

TRUTH ABOUT THE FUTURE

For every negative thought we have, someone else may be able to see the good that we no longer see or believe. The plans of our life, the totality of who we are, and what our life represents is yet to be determined. After a negative life experience, we can sometimes lose sight of who we are and what we believe about ourselves.

The beauty of who we are, and the totality of our value lies within, regardless of life's current circumstances.

Exercise Four: Read through the list below. Circle the things listed below that you believe about yourself.

I can experience love
I have value
My life is good
I can share my feelings
I am a positive person
I can accept help from others
I have gifts to share with others
I am beautiful.
I can heal
I am OK

I can find a new normal
I am intelligent
I have faith
People like me
I am safe
I can love myself
I can be healthy
I have hope
I have love to give
My life has purpose

The lies we sometimes tell ourselves, and sometimes even begin to believe, need to be brought into the light (discussed and dealt with) so that we can begin to see the truth about our life today. Believing in self and believing that life in general can get better is sometimes difficult. (These are dark periods in our lives.) Time and again throughout life it is good to examine ourselves; see what we believe, see that our life has value, see the gifts we can share with others, and see how our life continues to change. (Times we can see light, have hope.)

The plans of our life can be good and the person we choose to be can be positive.

Exercise Five: Place a STAR by any statement(s) in the above list that you hope to believe about yourself as you continue to move toward a new "right place" in life.

Place your hope in a brighter tomorrow by believing in yourself, the person you were created to be.

You are enough and are loved by the God who created you. You are His handiwork. (Ephesians 2:10)

 # ACKNOWLEDGING YOUR FEELINGS

Part of sharing life with one another means feeling safe enough to acknowledge and express our emotions. Our feelings are important. We all have emotional responses to situations and events we experience in life. These feelings need to be recognized and released as necessary. Recognizing, acknowledging, and expressing how we feel can sometimes help us to be able to process a negative life experience or a trial in life on an emotional level. Feelings can, and often do, change as time passes and healing begins. It is important to give ourselves time to feel and express our emotions, grieve if necessary, and heal as we work toward reconciling life.

Exercise One: Answer the following exercises based on how you feel about your life today.

1. **Place an "x" on the line to represent how angry you currently feel.**

←---→

Slightly   Very

2. **Place an "x" on the line to represent how sad you currently feel.**

←---→

Slightly   Very

3. **Place an "x" on the line to represent how depressed you currently feel.**

←---→

Slightly   Very

........FEELINGS CHANGE OVER TIME

The previous exercise is meant to be a self-evaluation regarding current personal feelings. The emotions, responses, and personal feelings someone has are just that, something someone can and should feel and express when necessary. No one feels or expresses emotions in exactly the same way.

Sometimes people do not feel they can experience complete recovery from traumatic events. Sometimes recovery, from certain situations and illnesses, is not possible. Reconciling, because it is a process, is one way we can start returning to a new "right place" at least on an emotional level.

Exercise Two: In the space below, write about your journey toward reconciling your feelings about negative life experiences or trials of life that have happened in the past, or that you might be currently experiencing. Think about how you felt initially, about your current feelings, and about your hope regarding future feelings. Write about how you see your life as you continue to reconcile toward a personal "right place".

_____

_____

_____

_____

... POSITIVE FEELINGS IN THE FUTURE

When we feel good about what we do and what our life represents, feelings about life itself may also begin to change too. There is no specific way to change how we feel about life, but we do have choices about how we approach life on a daily basis.

One choice is to look for the good around us, another choice is to do good for others when we can. Helping, and focusing on others sometimes helps us to see both the good we have in our lives and how we can impact others life for the good.

Exercise Three: Some people find that journaling, about something positive each day or about how they helped others that day, keeps the focus on seeing the positive in life. Write about a recent time you helped someone else and how the experience personally impacted you.

_____

_____

_____

_____

_____

SELF DEFENSE

Negative life events, trials, traumas and failures in life can happen. They may affect us directly or indirectly and impact us emotionally. Defense mechanisms are coping mechanisms we may use at times to help process life events on an emotional level. We may consciously or unconsciously use defense mechanisms in the moment or over an extended period of time.

Listed below are responses that are generally recognized as defense mechanisms. Read the ideas, examples and general explanations associated with each defense mechanism listed before completing the exercises.

Exercise One: Place a check by any or all defense mechanisms you use or have used in the past. Next, on the lines provided, write about a negative life experience, trial, trauma, or failure in life you associate with the defense mechanism you have used or are still using.

__DENIAL-a response in which someone will not admit that something sad, painful, etc. is true or real.

_____

__REPRESSION –a response process where distressing thoughts, memories, feelings of anxiety etc. are somehow temporarily moved from a conscious state to an unconscious state.

_____

__HUMOR-a response of laughter or amusement to an otherwise stressful situation. This response may also be expressed through sarcasm or joking.

_____

__BLAME-a response where someone thinks or says they believe that someone or something else is responsible for something that has happened.

_____

__TRIVIALIZE/MINIMIZE-a response in which someone tries to make something seem or appear less important or serious than it actually is.

_____

__ANGRY OUTBURST-a sudden verbal or physical response related to feelings of anger.

_____

Recognizing the defense mechanisms we use can be another part of reconciling something experienced in life. No one knows how long it takes for someone to reconcile a trial in life, a trauma of life, a failure in life, or a negative life event.

We can keep reconciling negative time periods in life sometimes by our self and sometimes with the help of others.

SELF-DOUBT AND NEGATIVE CHOICES

Sometimes negative life experiences can create or cause us to have self-doubt. Self-doubt can lead to feelings of insecurities about who we are and the choices we have. Recognizing how we respond to difficult situations, and realizing we have choices, may help us to be able to work toward a future we choose.

Exercise One: Check any or all statements you relate to. Write about the choices you know you have that can help you to make the best decisions for yourself in the future, by completing each statement.

___When I feel insecure, I often reject people before they can reject me. This pattern does not let others be a part of my life and keeps others from being able to help or show love towards me. In order to receive help and build relationships with others in the future I need to_____
_____.

___When I feel stressed, I turn to substances, food, sex or alcohol, as a means of coping with stressful situations. When I am feeling stressed, I can _____ instead of_____.

___Instead of dealing with my feelings of anger, I turn my anger inward and withdraw when I feel rejected. When I feel angry I can _____ instead of _____.

___Sometimes I am afraid to speak up when I am with a group of people. I am afraid someone will criticize me, my thoughts, or my opinions. The truth I know about myself is, I am_____ and my thoughts and opinions _____.

___I sometimes struggle with trying to change myself so that others will like me, instead of accepting myself for the person I am meant to be. The person I am is good enough, and accepting myself begins with _____.

___There are, and have been, times in my life when I no longer feel safe anywhere or with anyone. In order to begin to feel safe again I need to _____.

___When I am feeling anxious or nervous I often shut down instead of talking with people about what is going on. In order to deal with feeling anxious, or nervous around certain people, and in certain situations in the future I can_____.

___Because of past failed relationships, I struggle with trust. In order to build trust in my life again I need to_____.

___ I have a hard time setting clear boundaries. As a result, I allow others to use me or take advantage of me, often to my own detriment. Some boundaries I need to set with friends and family are _____
_____.

Finding someone we trust to talk to may help develop a support network and provide another layer of support.

Our future starts with each new day, deciding how we approach and live each day is a choice.

GRIEVING IS A PROCESS

When we suffer a significant loss in life, whether it is related to a person or an event, we may not always recognize our thoughts and feelings as being related to grief. Synonyms of the term grief are anguish, sorrow, or distress. Recognizing grief as a process with varying possible stages, may help normalize thoughts and feelings experienced as we grieve. While grieving, we may also begin to reconcile toward a new "right place" in life, over time and as we heal. The degree and length of time someone experiences grief is different. Grief is a personal process, with no exact order, absolute definition, or exact stages.

The following list are ideas and examples of responses (stages) related to a process of grieving. Read the ideas, examples and general explanations associated with the idea of viewing grief as a process.

Exercise One: Place a check by any responses/stages of grief you may identify with or may have personally experienced.

_____ **Shock/Denial/Disbelief**-A response of rejection regarding something unexpected. Something someone can't believe is actually real or true.

_____ **Emotional Reactions**-Expressed feelings. Emotional responses ranging from feeling no emotions to extreme emotional reactions with varying degrees in between.

_____ **Depression**-Described by some as feelings of aloneness and/or despair. These types of feelings could also be described by some people as "feeling" nothing.

_____ **Anxiousness**-Abnormal feelings or responses, also described by some as "not normal" feelings. Anxiousness can be expressed as a range of feelings from slight nervousness to feelings of panic.

_____ **Guilt**-The thought or ideas that something else, more or different, could have been done in a situation or event. Regret could also be associated with this type of response.

_____ **Anger/Resentment**-Negative feelings or reactions that could be experienced by some people when life does not match up to an expected or perceived reality.

_____ **Resisting Change**-An avoidance to moving forward. Also, could be described as feelings of worry or fear of acceptance of something different or new.

_____ **Hope-** A renewed feeling. This could be optimistic ideas or feelings about an unknown or unclear future.

_____ **Mindset Growth**-Looking toward, making plans and facing a new reality. Embracing the idea of change.

After a negative life experience or trial in life, people may go through any or all of the previously mentioned responses, reactions and suggested stages in no specific order and over no specific time period.

Grieving is a part of reconciling; it is part of the process of letting go and moving forward. We grieve over time and we heal individually, hopefully with help and love of friends and family.

HOLDING YOURSELF BACK

As stated in the introduction of this self-guided course, we don't always get to choose what happens in life. We do have choices about how we respond to what has happened. Life can be difficult. How we look at difficulties in life affects us personally, emotionally, socially, and even spiritually. **Personal issues** are something we may struggle and deal with. Some issues may resolve themselves and others we may reconcile over time. **Personal problems** need a solution. Some problems can be solved instantly, others take time. As stated previously, recognizing problems that need to be solved, and identifying issues that need reconciliation is part of the process of moving toward a new normal. We work through those problems and/or deal with issues sometimes by ourselves and sometimes with the help of others.

Exercise One: Circle any of the following categories or write in specific examples that relate to issues or problems you may be currently facing or might be currently ignoring.

Unresolved feelings   **Indecision**   **Negative behaviors**   **Disorders**   **Addictions**   **Unhealthy choices**

Grief   **Lack of forgiveness**   **Unhealthy relationships**   **Self-Doubt**   **Personal loss**   **Financial debt**

_____   _____   _____

Sometimes when we tell our self the truth about our life, it helps us begin to envision a new direction or develop a new attitude. A new vision or change in attitude can sometimes lead us toward a new truth about who we are, what our life represents, and a future we decide. Recognizing issues and problems, giving ourselves grace, seeking help, and setting goals are all a part of first step decisions. First step decisions help us start responding to things in life that may be personally affecting us in one way or another. (physically, emotionally, socially and spiritually)

Exercise Two: On the lines below write about the specific issues and problems relating to the categories you circled in the previous exercise. These are specific things that you realize you still need to take a first step toward addressing as you continue reconciling toward a new normal in life.

_____

_____

_____

_____

A new normal in life can sometimes begin with a change of heart, a change in life, and/or a change in how we view the future.

A life well lived in something we can all strive toward.

PROMISES OF THE FUTURE
"A bridge of love"

The future is waiting, it takes courage to cross a new bridge in life. When life doesn't turn out the way we thought it would, it takes strength from within (resilience) to keep moving forward.

We have all made promises we have not been able to keep. We have all been promised something and for one reason or another that promise wasn't kept. When promises do not come true, we may feel disappointed. Disappointments in life can cause us to feel pain and sometimes even despair. As we continue to move forward after experiencing a negative life event, trial or trauma in life, as stated in the first exercise, we may eventually experience post traumatic growth.

The strength, courage and endurance we develop can help us with personal growth. Loving yourself enough to want to move forward is part of personal growth. Crossing a bridge to the future may help us replace broken promises and negative life experiences with new thoughts, new life experiences and a brighter future never even imagined.

Crossing a bridge in love can mean committing to move forward, out of love of self, others and even life itself.

Exercise One: This is a journaling exercise. Answer the questions below thinking about broken promises and negative life experiences you have experienced. This journaling opportunity is your time for reflection as you attempt to cross a new bridge towards a life you plan. Write your response to the following questions by completing the statement.

What is different about the life you are currently living versus the life you thought you would be living by now? By now I thought...

_____

_____

_____

What broken promise(s), negative life experience(s) or trauma(s) have you gone through that may be keeping you from moving toward a new future? What I am working toward leaving behind...

_____

_____

_____

What does the future look like?   Write about the life you want to work toward living in the future; one you choose, one you make decisions about, one you start living today. In the future I will...

_____

_____

_____

_____

_____

_____

_____

_____

_____

Remember, most people face a time in their life when they make a choice to work toward leaving the past behind and crossing over towards a "right place" in the future. Deciding when and what that looks like is a choice for each of us.

The life we have been given is ours to live, sometimes by our self and sometimes with the help of others. Life is better together.

JOURNALING TOWARD HEALING

Sometimes we can't just move forward in life, we need a way to continue to process what is happening or has happened. Journaling is one way to look at the past, live in the present, while working through thoughts and emotions.

The benefits of journaling are:

- It provides us an opportunity to be honest with ourselves and about ourselves
- Allows us to safely recall what has happened
- Gives an us opportunity to look at the past, examine the present, and plan toward the future

Journaling does not have to be an extensive writing exercise it can be as simple as responding to statements, on a daily basis, that helps you to keep moving forward. Journaling allows us to **recall safely, realize life's realities gently, and reconcile slowly.** This self-guided course was created to allow individuals to do the same thing, just through an expanded process.

Exercise One: After completing the exercises in this course book, and on a daily basis, from that point forward you can begin journaling daily using the following lead-in statements as a starting point. On the lines below, practice journaling about events or moments in life you are currently reconciling. Write any thoughts you have that come to mind as you read each lead-in phrase.

I remember _____

_____

_____.

I realize I _____

_____

_____.

In the future I can _____

_____

_____.

Make or purchase your own journal so that you can *recall safely, realize gently, and reconcile slowly* for yourself anytime.

Sometimes being still starts an inward process toward renewing faith, regaining hope, and recognizing love even if it's only for one moment at a time.

EMOTIONAL HEALING

Being emotionally vulnerable during times of healing can sometimes be difficult but, allowing others to better understand our personal needs creates a better "help" environment for everyone.

The following exercise is meant to help you think about how you can help others who are trying to support you along your journey toward a "right place".

Exercise One: Think about the following scenarios and then answer the following statements. Write your answers on the lines below each statement

Expressing that we need time, space and even grace allows everyone to have a better understanding of what is currently going on. For example, if you state out loud, "I'm having a hard day and just need a little bit of time to myself" instead of "I'm done or I don't care", people have a better chance to express empathy toward you and your situation.

Words or phrases I can use or tell others that I am feeling emotionally stressed or vulnerable are:

_____

Having a "go to" statement can sometimes help us to emotionally detach from dealing with something in the moment. When we are feeling stressed, having a planned response or statement can help us to better express the feelings we may not be willing to talk about in that moment. For example, a "go to" statement could be "Right now is not the best time for me to..." or "Today is not the best day for me to deal with ...."

When I am having a bad day a respectful phrase that can be my "go to" statement is:

_____

Sometimes we can develop a sensitivity toward certain phrases; like when people tell us we are "ok" when we don't feel "ok". People who care about us don't usually intend to say hurtful things. By telling others about words or phrasing that bring back bad memories, sad thoughts or that momentarily cause us to shut down, helps ensure that those around us don't fail in the moment while trying to help.

A word or phrase that I am overly sensitive to, seems hurtful or I currently find offensive is:

_____

In life we may not always be well within our circumstances, but during all of life's circumstances we can choose to work toward being well within our soul.

A LIFE YOU CHOOSE TO LIVE

There are no guarantees of a perfect life. As stated throughout this course many times, negative events, failures, and traumas happen. How we choose to live our life from that point forward is a choice we make over time.

We can begin to reconcile life, time and again by; knowing the truth about our life, healing throughout life, living one day at a time.

Thinking about all of the exercises you have worked through, if your life was a pencil what type of pencil would you be?

- **Broken**, choosing not to move forward after a negative life experience.
- **Half of a broken pencil**, barely engaging in life, not connected, only recognizing that you are broken but not doing anything to begin to heal.
- **Barely mended**, a scotch taped life, one that from the outside looks mended. Surface healing at most.
- **"Normal"**, glued back together, moving forward after a negative life experience, taking one day at a time as they come, being real about your situation and still looking toward hope.
- **Stronger than ever**, repaired better than new, visibly healed scars, experiencing post traumatic growth on a regular basis. Thriving, scars and all, living with a realization that life will never be the same, but it is always worth the effort it takes to keep living a full life.

Exercise One: Place a check beside the type of pencil your life currently represents after considering the following statement.

The life I have been living because of my negative life experiences, or traumas in life is:

__ Broken

__ Half

__ Barely Mended

__ "Normal"

__ Stronger Than Ever

The life I want to begin living as I continue to reconcile life in the future:

__ Broken   __ Half Life   __ Barely Mended

__ "Normal"   __ Stronger Than Ever

We never know how strong we are until strength is all we have left.

 # LIVING A BALANCED LIFE

We live a balanced life as we strive to be socially connected, emotionally healthy, physically fit, intellectually challenged and spiritually fed. After a negative life experience, or trauma in life, sometimes we may feel like our life is out of balance.

Exercise One: Read through each statement that refers to areas of life mentioned in the previous paragraph. Write your answers to the statements on the lines below as you strive toward living a life that is more balanced in the future.

Socially connected. We can build healthy relationships by engaging and participating in a community of relationships. Developing and maintaining friendships can provide physical and emotional support long term.

In the future I can meet people and build friendships as I...

_____

Emotionally healthy. Negative life experiences can affect us emotionally. Our mind and heart may sometimes need to refresh and heal. We need to take time for ourselves and do things that refresh us emotionally.

In order to refresh and sometimes emotionally heal, I need to...

_____

Physically fit. Taking care of our body helps protect our future health. Eating properly and exercising are part of self-care. Our physical health impacts many other parts of our lives including our ability to be active and do things with others.

Over the next year the changes I want to make to improve my physical health are...

_____

Intellectually challenged. Learning and growing as an individual is something we can do our entire life. When and how we grow, in part, depends on the effort we put forth, the pathways of life we choose, the goals we set, and the decisions we personally make.

To grow as a person, I need to ...

_____

Spiritually fed. Our personal core values, what we believe, are also important to our overall well-being as they are matters of the mind and heart. *Growing* in love, *renewing* faith, and *restoring* hope are some of the ways we continue to develop on a spiritual level.

In regard to my spiritual life, I grow, renew, and restore best by...

_____

UNCONDITIONAL LOVE
I CORINTHIANS 13: 4-8 ADAPTED

Love is patient, love is kind.

Love does not envy, does not boast, it is not proud.

Love does not dishonor others, it is not self-seeking. Love is not easily angered.

Love keeps no record of wrong.

Love does not delight in evil.

Love rejoices in truth.

Love always protects, trusts, hopes, and perseveres.

Love never fails

LOVE RESTORES

Up until now this self-guided course has touched on a few topics involving words, attitudes and actions that show love. Three things remain throughout life; faith, hope, and love. With the greatest of these being love. **Love is powerful.**

Focusing on what love is and is not helps us to learn more about love of self and love of others. Since love itself never fails or ends, reconciling through love can be an ongoing process throughout life. Love always protects, trusts, hopes, and perseveres. Living out love is about choosing to love ourselves and others through our words and by our actions. **Actions of Love restore.**

Exercise One: Write your answers to the following questions on the lines below each question.

I Corinthians 13:4-8 is an example of how we can live out the concepts of love in word and action. As you reconcile your negative life experiences which of the concepts found in I Corinthians 13:4-8 helps or encourages you personally?

_____

_____

Relationships need to be built and rebuilt around actions that show love. Which concepts of love do you struggle to accept or show toward others because of what you have been through?

_____

_____

Out of love for yourself and those who love you, which concepts shared in I Corinthians 13 do you want to work toward showing more to others through your words and actions as you continue to heal and reconcile throughout life?

_____

_____

Love yourself enough, and those who love you, to keep reconciling through all of life's circumstances. You can read more about love by purchasing the book ***Love Forever*** written by Bretta Durham through the website RealLifeRelationships.org or from Amazon.com.

 # LOVE RECONCILES

Taking life experiences through an educational process such as this self-guided course can sometimes be helpful in the process of reconciling life toward a "right place". Matters of the heart (our spiritual life) are not something we may be able to completely deal with by ourselves.

If you feel you need to reconcile matters of the heart (spiritual matters), or need to find a new "right place" along your spiritual journey in life, keep reading.

Reconciling through love can mean taking anything to God. Jesus tells us in Matthew 11:28 that we can come to him when we are weary and burdened. Again, when we are weak he makes us strong by His grace as told in 2 Corinthians 12:9. Colossians 1:19-20 tells us all things have been reconciled through the blood of Christ. We are told He renews us in Psalms 103:2-5. There isn't anything we have done, or anything that has happened, that God doesn't already know about or can't understand. Taking negative life events and traumas in life to God is a choice we make in our own time. He patiently waits, His love never fails, and He can make all things new by restoring us spiritually time and again.

Exercise One: Write your answers to the following question on the lines below.

Is there anything you need God to help you deal with that you don't feel you can reconcile or heal from without divine help?

_____

_____

A relationship with God is always available to us. Nothing can separate us from the love of God as told in Romans 8:37-39. Unconditional love starts with God, for God is love according to 1 John 4:8. The book of 1 John talks about the Christian life, all that God has done for us and the life He offers to us. Deciding when you want to talk about your spiritual journey is up to you.

Help through love is available to you, to set you free, to let you live, and to let you love.

God loved us first. He knows our past, present and future. John 3:16 describes how we enter into a relationship with Jesus Christ. A relationship with Christ is available to all who are willing to recognize and acknowledge Him as their personal savior.

Exercise Two: Place a check by any or all statements you are interested in considering.
___ I would like someone to pray for me.
___ I want to talk to someone about unconditional love of God available to me.
___ I would like a copy of *Loved First* to learn more about God's unconditional love and the relationship with God that is available to me. Contact Bretta through RealLifeRelationships.org to receive *Loved First*.

Reconciling Through ♥

Looking at past negative life events, while

Opening your heart, mind and soul to healing in the present.

Valuing yourself and the parts of your life still yet to be lived,

Enough to find FAITH, HOPE and LOVE again in the future.

Real Life Relationships goal for this self-guided course is for people to have an opportunity to reconcile relationships and life toward a new "right place" over time. Real Life Relationships self-guided courses help people to *Learn Connect Love.*

As an individual or couple you can continue to

- **RECALL negative life events safely in your own time**
- **REALIZE life's realities gently as you look toward the future**
- **RECONCILE slowly to a "right place"**

Jeremiah 29:11 God has a plan for your future, His plans are good.

Ephesians 2:10 You are God's handiwork, your life has value.

I Corinthians 13 God is love and His concepts of love are unconditional.

John 3:16 God loved us first, He knows our past, present and future. He desires to have a relationship with us throughout our entire life, regardless of life's current circumstances.

James 2:2-4, Romans 5:1-5, 1 Corinthians 13:4, 2 Corinthians 12:9, Ephesians 2:10

Note: If you received this self-guided course as a gift you may want to pay it forward. Your gift would allow another individual to benefit from this course as well. Real Life Relationships is a nonprofit company dedicated to helping people to *Learn Connect Love.* Visit **RealLifeRelationships.org** to donate $25 so that another individual can receive a copy of **"Reconciling Through Love".**

To learn about other self-guided courses offered, to order the book ***Love Forever*** directly, or if you need additional information about services offered visit our website **RealLifeRelationships.org.**

If you purchased this self-guided course yourself and would like to purchase additional copies visit our website **RealLifeRelationships.org** or Amazon.com.

NOTES

NOTES